DIY Eas Guide to Making Scented Soy & Beeswax Candles and Wax Melts at Home

Learn to Make Seasonal & Healing Candles with Aromatherapy Blends

By

Ally Russell

CONTENTS

INTRODUCTION

Do you remember the fresh smell of spring? How about the warm summer breeze or the cozy winter holiday season? Every season has its distinct aroma that we can all identify them easily with.

Candles are wonderful and versatile items. Not only are they relatively simple to make, but the range of colors and scents you can choose to make them in is only limited by your imagination.

You can choose scents to match a season and give as gifts– sweet fresh cream and lavender in spring, a subtle combination of cut grass and rain for summer, cinnamon with just a dash of cloves during autumn, a cup of thick hot chocolate covered in marshmallows for the winter holidays.

Whether you are feeling uncharacteristically blue, stressed, or uncomfortable by a stuffy smell, you can choose scents that match a specific design or mood for a room. You can even mix specific scents to help with certain health problems. A few of these would include mint, rosemary, chamomile, and thyme, or honeysuckle.

In this book, we're going to look at the basics of making candles and the types you can make, how to melt wax, how to place the wick properly; all the technicalities involved in the trade. There will also be a quick discussion of what a scent throw is– both hot and cold– and how to compare them.

Then we'll discuss how you can combine certain oils and essences in order to develop the right blend of unique fragrances that apply to you and your potential customers.

In no time, you'll be ready to go to make your own candles in any variety of scents and colors of your choice for any occasion. So let's get started! Shall we?

TINY BIT OF HISTORY LESSON FOR YOU

Here is a little bit of boring history lesson for you (in case anyone ever asks if you know the history of candle making).

With such a rich and traditional history of being used for birthday celebrations, religious services, holidays, home decorations, and even as the only source of artificial light during the old days, candles used to be made from tallow.

This material is extracted from sheep and various cattle during the Roman and early Egyptian times, and while they served their purpose at the time, they burned terribly and were inefficient.

During the Middle Ages, candles began to be made from beeswax for religious and worship purposes, which was indeed a drastic improvement but can be quite expensive in its limited quantity. Candles were thus made available only for the upper class and members of the clergy.

Early settlers in colonial America soon discovered that they could boil berries from the bay-berry shrub and produce a sweet-smelling candle, but as the process is tedious and inefficient as well, candle making using this kind of process just wasn't practical. By the 18th century, the rise of the whaling industry gave birth to the widespread availability of whale oil.

Whale oil could now be used as a good replacement for tallow, beeswax, and bayberry wax, but the smell of the oil was rather unpleasant.

When the 19th century rolled around, the first patented candle making machines arrived along with braided wicks, as well as new research and discoveries from chemists Michael Eugene Chevreul and Joseph Gay Lussac.

Paraffin wax began to be commercially produced—it burned clean and bright and had no unpleasant odor. Cheaper and sturdier candles were then manufactured from paraffin wax and stearic acid.

Today, a wide variety of materials can be used to create candles—beeswax, soy, vegetable waxes, gel waxes, and so much more. In the market today, candles can be broken down into different categories, some of which include the following: container candles are poured into special containers like tan, glass, or pottery.

They are usually for decorative purposes and can have different fragrances added to them. Votive candles are freestanding and usually white and unscented. They are used for gratitude or devotion, usually in religious events and ceremonies.

Taper candles, from their name alone, are very slender and can have heights of up to 20" in total. Tea light candles, on the other hand, are very small and are usually placed in cylindrical aluminum or polycarbonate holders.

There are plenty of colors and fragrances to choose from as well, and we'll get to the nitty-gritty of every single detail in the pages to come.

So sit back, put on your thinking cap on, and let's get started.

SUPPLIES YOU NEED

Candle making equipment and tools can vary, depending on the type of candles you make, but some basic tools and equipment are necessary for making any type of candles. It's best to gather all your equipment ahead of time and organize it. Doing so ensures that you have everything you need for a successful candle-making session.

Having your supplies and equipment available and organized can also make candle making safer. Candle making requires your focus and presence, so it's not safe to leave the work area during the candle-making process to look for supplies or equipment. Lack of organization in the work area can result in accidents or botched batches of candles. You don't want either!

Since candles are all about the wax and wicks, let's start there. As I said before, the goal of this book is to provide information on natural candles, so the focus is on beeswax and soy wax.

WAX

Of course, when you start any worthwhile endeavor, you need to arm yourself with the right tools and equipment for your so-called battle ahead. Wax is one of the most important supplies you need in your candle making business, and we've spent quite a big part of the beginning of this book talking about the different kinds of natural waxes available to you.

The traditional wax that candle makers have been using since forever is the paraffin wax. It's still the most popular and most widely available commercial wax on the market today, and for a good reason. It's cheap and easily purchasable but contains harmful toxic ingredients and chemicals.

Soy is a natural alternative to paraffin wax, made from soybean oil and is longer lasting, burns cleaner, and is easier to clean.

Beeswax is the oldest candle making wax, produced by bees, and is a hundred percent natural. On the plus side, it's totally chemical-free; on the downside, it is also much more expensive and harder to come by.

Soy Wax

Soy wax is a clean-burning, eco-friendly, sustainable wax that is made from the oil of soybeans. Soybean crops are major crops in the United States in Indiana, Illinois, and Iowa. Once the soybeans are harvested, they go through a process of being cleaned, cracked, and hulled.

Then, they are formed into flakes, and the oil is removed from the flakes. To make the oil solid at room temperature, the oil goes through a hydrogenation process that changes some of the fatty acids in the oil from unsaturated to saturated.

There are various types of soy wax. One-hundred percent soy wax is what most people prefer if they are concerned about burning clean candles with no toxic emissions. Pure soy wax is usually used for container candles as the melting point is lower than a soy-blend wax.

Soy wax is known as a one-pour or single-pour wax, meaning it is soft enough that it won't shrink after it is poured into the container and hardens, and therefore, the wax won't release and leave a gap between the container and the candle.

When making pillar candles or taper candles, often a soy blend wax is used for the benefit of the candle becoming hard enough to stand on its own without a container.

Some soy candle manufacturers claim that soy candles burn 50% longer than candles of the same size made from paraffin, depending on the environment in which they are burned and how they are stored.

Soy wax is white in color and can be purchased in convenient pellet or flake form. When planning the colors of your candles, it's important to realize that soy wax doesn't accept dye as readily as paraffin, and your candles will be lighter in color than if paraffin is used.

For instance, it may be difficult to get a deep red or green for winter holiday candles. One of the beauties of soy candles is the softer, natural colors.

Beeswax can be purchased in various kinds, and the quality of the wax can vary. It's important that you know which beeswax is right for any specific candle-making project. Here are some types of beeswax that you should know.

Brood wax is the lowest quality of beeswax. This is the beeswax that was used in the beehive to house bee larvae.

Because the wax is often left in the beehive for several seasons so the bees don't have to create a new honeycomb before they can lay eggs, the wax becomes darkened from the honey and other stuff that is left behind in it.

When brood wax is used for making candles or other projects, you must first melt it, adding a little water, so the impurities will sink to the bottom of the melting container and can be strained out. Unfortunately, this process causes much of the wax to be wasted.

CAPPING WAX

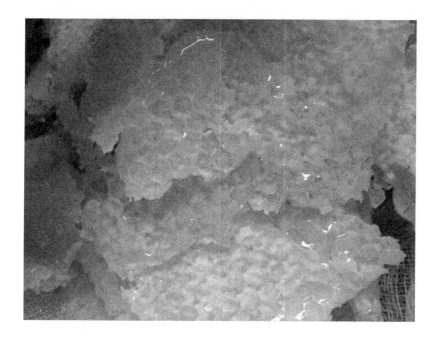

Capping wax is a commonly used, golden wax for candles. It is fairly clean but should be rendered, without water, before making candles because it may contain bits of bee parts or honey.

Before using, melt the capping wax, and let it sit in the container over a warming candle or other gentle heat source for about an hour while the debris settles at the bottom of the container. Pour the yellow wax on the top into a mold. When it hardens, it's ready to melt for candle-making.

CLEANED YELLOW BEESWAX

Cleaned yellow beeswax is more expensive than capping wax, but you do not need to render it before using it and, thus, it is usually considered the best type of beeswax for making candles.

WHITE BEESWAX

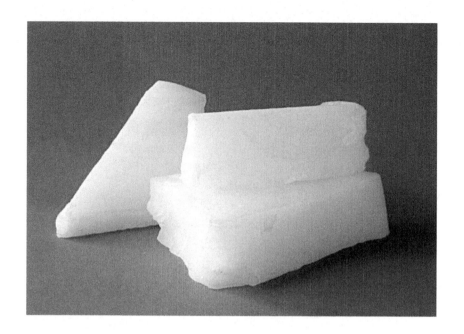

White beeswax is the purest and most expensive type of beeswax as it contains no debris or honey. White beeswax is pure from filtering through a carbon filter, or it is bleached by UV light treatment.

WHERE TO FIND AND BUY BEESWAX

There are various places where beeswax can be purchased, or you can gather your own beeswax if you should decide to keep bees. If keeping bees isn't your thing, but you want "fresh from the hive" beeswax, check with local beekeepers that might have beeswax for sale.

You may be able to locate a beekeeper in your area by visiting the American Beekeeping Federation website: http://www.abfnet.org/ or at *Bee Culture, The Magazine of American Beekeeping* website at http://www.beeculture.com/find-local-beekeeper/

WICK

The size or the width of the wick is the most important factor to consider. Large wicks are usually best for container candles that have a diameter of a few inches. The experienced candle makers know the wick is the most important part of the candle. Even if the candle wax is perfect, the candle will not burn properly without the correct wick.

Wicking for candles comes in various sizes and is often made from cotton, paper, zinc, or wood. The correct type and size of the wicking are based on what type of wax is used for the candle, the diameter of the candle, and the environment in which the candle will be burned (drafty, indoor, or outdoor, etc.).

You need a wick that creates a consistent flame size and a well-formed wax pool without dripping down the side of the candle.

The wick needs to be big enough to draw liquid wax into the flame before it drips down the candle, but small enough to melt only a small pool of wax, so the wick doesn't become flooded with too much wax.

WICKS FOR BEESWAX CANDLES

Finding the right wick for beeswax candles can be a little more difficult than for paraffin wax because there are so many variables in beeswax, such as geographic location, when the wax was harvested, and how it was harvested.

You can follow the general guidelines for beeswax candle wicks but always be aware of the variables in beeswax when making candles, and adjust if necessary.

Candle wicks include the following types: cored, square, and flat wicks.

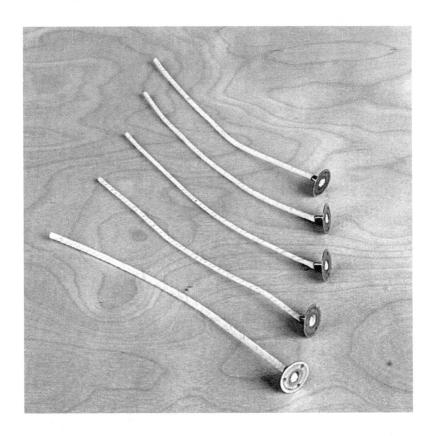

CORED WICKS

Cored wicks have a stiff core made of wire, cotton, or paper. They are often used for votive candles, jar candles, and tea light candles. These wicks are usually purchased already cut to length and with a wick tab attached.

The wick tab is the small round or square-shaped piece of metal found at the end of the wick to help the wick "stand up" in the container. Cored wicks burn hotter so the wax can be completely burned.

SQUARE WICKS

Square wicks are the sturdiest type of wicks and are premium wicks for using with beeswax taper and pillar candles.

FLAT WICKS

Flat wicks are braided with three bundles of fiber and are usually used for paraffin candles but clog easily and are not as suitable for beeswax candles.
The size of the wick must be correct for the diameter of the candle.

If the wick is too large, it will smoke as the flame will consume the wax too fast. The candle will also flicker if the wick is too large. If the wick is too small, it cannot burn the wax fast enough, and the wax will pool and drip.

To get just the right size wick, start with a recommended size for the wax type and candle diameter, and conduct tests with different wicks in that size range to see if that is the best size for a specific candle. Sample packages of wicks or small packages of each size are sold by many candle-making suppliers so you can experiment without purchasing large packages of one size.

Every variation can change the way the candle burns and what size wick is needed, including how much fragrance or color is added to the wax and the diameter of the candle container. To test wick sizes, make six of the exact same candles, placing a different size wick in each candle. Label each candle container with the wick size (use a dark marker and write in large print on the label) used for that candle.

Line up the candles on a table or counter and make sure the label is clearly visible or tape an additional note to the table in front of each candle. Light the candles. As they burn, every hour, take a digital photo of the group of candles, making sure you capture the top of each candle so you can check the melt pool.

When the candle has burned one hour for each inch of the candle at its widest point, check the melt pool.

The candle should have a one-half inch melt pool if the wick is the correct size. If the candle has a melt pool smaller than one-half inch, the wick is too small.

If the candle has a melt pool that is more than three-fourths inch, the wick is too large.

Cotton Wick Guide

WICK	BURN
UC WICK 1.593 (TEALIGHT)	4.0cm
UC WICK 1.699 (TEALIGHT)	4.3cm
UC WICK 1.300 A	3.3cm
UC WICK 1.375	3.5cm
UC WICK 1.450	3.7cm
UC WICK 1.600	4.1cm
UC WICK 1.651	4.2cm
UC WICK 1.705	4.3cm
UC WICK 1.792	4.6cm
UC WICK 1.832	4.7cm
UC WICK 2.000	5.1cm
UC WICK 2.076	5.3cm
UC WICK 2.164	5.5cm
UC WICK 2.283	5.8cm
UC WICK 2.300	5.8cm
UC WICK 2.402	6.1cm
UC WICK 2.592	6.6cm
UC WICK 2.672	6.8cm
UC WICK 2.775	7.0cm
UC WICK 2.900	7.4cm
UC WICK 2.950	7.5cm
UC WICK 3.000	7.6cm
UC WICK 3.100	7.9cm

WOODEN WICK CHART

Wooden Wick Guide

WICK	BURN
WOODEN WICK SIZE 1	6.5cm to 7.4cm
WOODEN WICK SIZE 2	7.5cm to 8.4cm
WOODEN WICK SIZE 3	8.5cm - 9.4cm
WOODEN WICK SIZE 4	9.5cm -10cm
MORE THAN 10CM	2 WICKS RECOMMENDED

https://craftycandlesupplies.com.au/wick_guide_ch oosing_the_best_wicks_for_your_soy_candles/

WOODEN WICKS

Last but not least, let's not forget the wooden wicks. As customers seek out natural-looking candles, wooden wicks have become quite popular. Some wooden wicks are manufactured in such a way to create a "crackling" sound when burned, like when a fireplace log burns and crackles.

The crackling sound adds to the ambiance of the room.

While wooden wicks are not suitable for beeswax candles, they can be used in soy wax container candles. (Wooden wicks should not be used in votives or pillars.) The recommendation for the wooden wicks size for pure soy candles is the large or extra-large size.

E-Z WICK SETTING TOOL

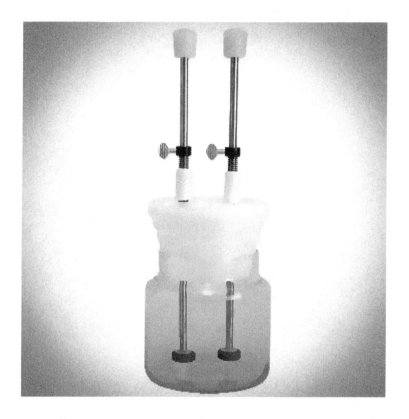

This is an excellent tool that ensures you get perfectly centered wicks in your jars. It works by automatically centering and setting the wick into the container of your choice. The tool works with all possible container sizes.

It is easily adjustable between all various diameter sizes. Though this is not a must-have for making candles, but trust me when I say it will make the experience much easier and fun.

This is all you need to get started with making candles. Next, let's take a look and see what equipment you will need to get started with.

EQUIPMENT GUIDE

DOUBLE BOILER

A double boiler a tool that has one pot inside another little larger pot, you fill up the outer pot with water and inner pot with wax. Once you put it on a stove top, the water warms up, in turn, melts the wax. It is the safest way to melt your wax evenly.

A typical double boiler should cost you not more than $40

You can also use a true double boiler or a universal boiler that you can use on top of any of your pots readily available at home. This candle making must keep you from melting the wax directly over your flame source.

Make sure that your double boiler can fit in your cupboard as well. As for your containers for the candles, you can use anything from glassware, coffee mugs, mason jars, and anything that you believe can withstand the heat of the candle.

POURING POT

Just as the name implies, the pouring pot is what is used to melt the wax and pour the melted wax into the molds or containers. For the best results, select a pot that is sturdy with an easy-grip handle and pouring spout.

Pouring pots range in size, but a good size is a three-quart size that holds about four pounds of wax.

Most pouring pots are made from aluminum and cost between $10 to around $25. Some candle makers prefer to own a pouring pot for each scent they frequently use, so the scent from the previous batch of candles does not transfer to the current batch of wax.

THERMOMETER

Another useful tool in candle making is the thermometer. This will help you take the temperature of the wax when you're in the middle of your candle recipe—just be sure to follow the instructions in your wax bundle as to which temperature to add fragrance, to pour into your chosen container, and the like.

You can then use a spoon or a spatula to break up wax chunks and stir the wax into an even consistency.

Precision in quantities is essential for consistency in the candles. A good digital or analog scale allows you to weigh ingredients and record the weight of what you used so you can repeat your successes without guesswork.

A digital scale is quick and easy to read, taking the guesswork out of reading the scale accurately. A digital scale is more expensive than an analog scale, but the difference may be made up in fewer mistakes that contribute to the waste of supplies and time.

MOLDS & CONTAINER

Molds come in a variety of shapes and sizes and are made from various materials such as silicone and aluminum. If you enjoy making one-of-a-kind candles, you can create molds out of various household materials such as small waxed juice containers.

The important thing to remember about molds is that you must be able to release the candle from the mold without breaking the candle.

Glass jars of various types are the typical container of choice for container candles when making them in large numbers; however, you can use interesting containers such as small plant pots, tins, small wooden boxes, interesting cups, etc. Be sure whatever container used will not break from the heat of the candle.

Here are some of my recommended stores that you can check out when you are shopping for your candle making tools and equipment, but please understand, I am not anyway associated or an affiliate for any of these businesses.

Also, most online retailers do change often, so at the time you read this, I highly recommend you do your own research on Google and see which online retailers are coming up on top and who is offering the best prices and free shipping.

- Candle Supplies at General Wax & Candle Company
- Bitter Creek Candle Supplies
- Discount Candle Supplies
- MillCreek Soy Wax Candle Supplies
- Nature's Garden Wholesale Candle & Candle Supplies

CANDLE-MAKING SAFETY

MELTING WAX

While wax-melting may seem like an easy and simple step, it is, in fact, one of the most dangerous parts of making candles at home. There are some safety precautions you should make sure you take each time you make a batch of candles, so this way you can avoid the majority of hazards involved.

The first and most important thing is always to make sure you have a fire extinguisher within easy reach. Familiarize yourself with the proper operation of a fire extinguisher by reading the instructions on it. While you'll likely never need to use it if you follow proper safety measures, you don't want to find yourself needing to read instructions while a fire spreads rampantly across your house.

If you are dealing with small wax fires, then using something small like a pot lid will help smother the fire before is spreads. Never apply water to a wax fire, though. Liquid wax acts similar to oil so you should treat it as an oil fire, and if you were to throw water into an oil fire, not only would the fire spread, but the water would bounce right back on your exposed skin.

Next, it is very important that you never leave melting wax unattended. While it may take a while for the wax to go from a solid to a liquid, you should never walk away from it, even for a single second. Once wax becomes a liquid, the temperature rises sharply.

This is why you must constantly monitor the temperature of the wax; once it reaches its flashpoint above 300 degrees Fahrenheit, the vapors are going to be highly flammable. Take note never to allow the batches of wax to reach a temperature higher than their flashpoint, or there will definitely be several dangers.

You should always use a double boiler when it comes to melting wax. This will help distribute the heat evenly and prevent you wax from reaching the dangerous flashpoint temperatures we discussed. Wax should never be melted directly on the stove or it will burn and potentially cause a fire.

If possible, you should always use an electric heat source or a very stable flame out of reach of any air drafts. That way, if your wax accidentally reaches its flashpoint then it is less likely the vapors will find a flame and ignite. Any open flame, such as a gas burner, will ignite wax vapors.

Lastly, always make sure you use a thermometer to monitor the temperature of your wax. If you don't have a thermometer, you should get one before you start making candles of your own.

BAIN-MARIE SET UP

Let's talk about two specific vocabulary terms for a moment. A double boiler requires a water pot of simmering water and a container larger than the circumference of that pot on top of it. The bottom of that container should never touch the surface of the water in the pot below, and the water being heated should never actually reach boiling temperature.

A typical way of melting chocolate, for instance, is to use a double boiler consisting of a water pot and a larger heat-proof container with the chocolate inside; the steam coming from the water heats the chocolate and melts it in a gentle way that is easy to control.

Now, a bain-marie takes both of those rules and purposely breaks them. For one, a bain-marie still involves a pot filled with one or two inches of water, but the second container or saucepan should be smaller than the water pot. This happens so that the second container is surrounded by boiling water, quickly melting whatever is inside.

Candle-making requires the bain-marie method, so do remember the difference between both terms. In this case, the water temperature will never get over 212 degrees Fahrenheit. You will place the pouring pot with wax within the boiling water of a larger pot.

The boiling water transfers heat to the pouring pot so that your wax doesn't get scorched and the risk of fire is reduced. Even if you are melting wax with this safer arrangement, you should still never leave it unattended.

The basic steps for melting your wax and setting up a bain-marie system are as follows:

1. Choose an old pot that is large enough to hold your pouring pot.
2. Add an inch or two of water to the old pot.
3. Bring the water to a boil.
4. Place the pouring pot directly into the boiling water. You can also place a metal cookie cutter

or another similar item in the bottom of the old pot to elevate the pouring pot.

5. Lower the heat, so the water simmers. You don't need to maintain a rapid boil. Both produce the same temperature of 212 degrees Fahrenheit.

6. Remember to occasionally add water to replace any evaporated parts. Never let the bain-marie run out of water since it will get too hot very quickly.

7. Allow your wax to melt and monitor the temperature until you reach the desired temperature needed for the specific type of wax you are working with.

CANDLE MAKING PROCESS

Typical Candles have four main ingredients

- Wax
- wick
- Color
- Fragrance

SEVEN STEPS TO MAKING CANDLES SUCCESSFULLY AT HOME

STEP 1: MEASURE THE WAX

Here is the general formula that you should follow when you are choosing the amount of wax against your container:

The volume of the container in ml X the number of containers X 0.85 = Your Soy Wax in grams

Do not forget to take the lid of your container into consideration. Leave an approximate of about half a centimeter as a gap between the lid and the surface of the wax if your candle container has a lid. Remember that this space will be allotted for your wick so that it can stand when the container is closed!

STEP 2: MELT THE WAX

Use a double boiler to heat the wax to the appropriate temperature. If you need to create a double boiler, you can put about an inch of water in a saucepan and then place the pouring pot in the water. You should add an inexpensive metal trivet or cookie cutter under the pouring pot to elevate it.

When you do this, you will ensure the wax doesn't get direct heat on any side. Then adjust the heat to a medium-low setting.

The water needs to boil, but shouldn't be a rolling boil. Water that is at a rolling boil may splatter out of the pan. Occasionally check the temperature of the wax to ensure it isn't getting too hot. Keep adjusting the temperature as needed and never leave the wax unattended.

STEP 3: MEASURE AND ADD FRAGRANCE OIL

Normally, for a soy wax candle, you should add about 6-10% grams of fragrance oil to your soy wax. Here is a general formula for the amount of fragrance oil that you need:

Soy wax in grams X 0.10 = Fragrance Oil in ml

Remember, the fragrance is best measured by weight, but you can also use a tablespoon to measure it if you don't have a scale that measures small amounts precisely. A tablespoon equals 0.5 ounces. Stir the wax after adding the fragrance oil.

STEP 4: MEASURE AND ADD DYE

We will talk more about colors, mixing hues, and the color wheels further on in more detail, but for now, what you need to know is that more wax equals more dye and that you need more dye to achieve darker colors.

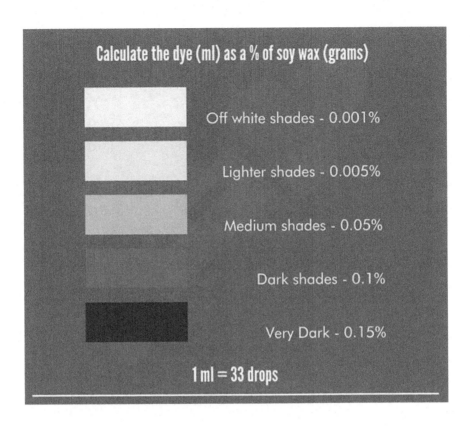

Calculate the dye (ml) as a % of soy wax (grams)

Off white shades - 0.001%

Lighter shades - 0.005%

Medium shades - 0.05%

Dark shades - 0.1%

Very Dark - 0.15%

1 ml = 33 drops

Here is what you need to know regarding calculating how much liquid colored dyes you will need:

Amount of wax in grams X Liquid dye percentage = Liquid Dye per Candle in ml

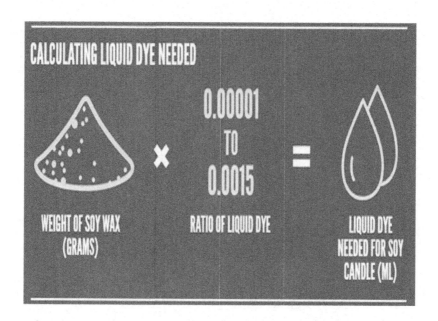

CALCULATING LIQUID DYE NEEDED

WEIGHT OF SOY WAX (GRAMS) × RATIO OF LIQUID DYE (0.00001 TO 0.0015) = LIQUID DYE NEEDED FOR SOY CANDLE (ML)

Image sources:

https://craftycandlesupplies.com.au/media/wysiwyg/Guides/Dye-guide/Liquid-Dye.jpg

STEP 5: TEST THE COLOR

The liquid wax will often appear darker than once it is completely cooled. To test your coloring, drip a small amount of wax onto a paper plate or towel, being careful not to drip anything on your hands.

Allow it to harden, and you can see an adequate representation of what the candle color will look like. If needed you can then add more dye.

STEP 6: ADD UV STABILIZER (OPTIONAL)

This is the time you can add UV Stabilizer if you want. If you choose to add this, you will prevent the color from fading when the candles are exposed to UV rays or fluorescent lighting. You typically add about 1/2 teaspoon per pound of wax.

STEP 7: MIX INGREDIENTS

Remove the pouring pot using something to protect your hand since the handle may have heated up slightly. You may want to set it on some paper towels first to absorb the water from the double boiler. You're now ready to pour your wax.

HOT WAX SAFETY

Before you begin working with wax overheat, you must be aware that each type of wax has a *flashpoint*. The flashpoint of wax is the temperature at which the wax will start to burn and flame.

The flashpoint typically varies from between 250 degrees to 400 degrees, but since the flashpoint is different for various types of wax, it's important that you get the flashpoint information directly from the manufacturer of the wax you are using.

It's also critical that you always use a thermometer when melting the wax. You may be able to "eye it" to some extent, but it's risky not to use a thermometer.

If you do not know the flashpoint for the wax you are using, you are at risk for the wax getting too hot and flaming during the melting process.
This can quickly lead to a major fire in your workspace. (There is more information on wax flashpoints, melt points, and pour points in the chapter on making candles.) Always know the flashpoint and never heat the wax beyond the flashpoint!

If your wax does reach the flashpoint and you have a fire on your hands, *do not use water to extinguish the fire.*

Pouring water on the fire will make the flames soar. Instead of water, use a fire extinguisher to put out the fire. If you do not have a fire extinguisher, though it's recommended that you keep one in the workspace, use sand, baking soda, or flour to put out the flames.

MAKING CONTAINER CANDLES

A container candle is basically a non-flammable container that is filled with wax and has a wick at the center. There are several reasons why these types of candles are so popular. First, these offer you a candle and candle holder in one so you don't have to worry about dripping wax.

Second, when making container candles, you can use a lower melting point wax that offers you a stronger scent. This means you'll be able to cast a more evident scent than a free-standing candle.

There are also numerous ways to make container candles. However, in this book, I'm going to give you the most basic and simple steps to making them.

You can choose various waxes for your container candles, and you may need to adjust this basic recipe depending on the specific type of wax you are using. This recipe is for using straight general-purpose paraffin wax.

For this basic recipe you'll need the following:

- ☐ Wax suitable for container candles.
- ☐ Any desired colors or fragrance oils.
- ☐ Containers suitable for candles such as heat-proof ceramics or glassware, and tins.
- ☐ A bain-marie set up to melt the wax.
- ☐ Pre-tabbed wicks of a suitable size that matches the diameter of your container.

- ☐ Hot glue from either a hot glue gun or a hot glue pot.
- ☐ Bic Pen.
- ☐ Clothespins.
- ☐ Thermometer.
- ☐ Heat Gun.

The process:

Step 1: Prepare the wax mixture.

While your wax is melting with the bain-marie, you can take the time to review the rest of the instructions. The ideal target temperature for melting wax is 170 to 175 degree Fahrenheit.

After the wax is melted entirely, you can stir in any additives you want such as color dyes and a few drops of fragrance. Remember to not include too much of it, since these are concentrated scents intended to be used in small quantities. You should add them in the following order:

1. Additives like stearic acid.
2. Fragrance oil.

3. Color dyes.

While your wax is melting, you can continue onto the next several steps, but always monitor your wax temperature closely.

Step 2: Add wicks to the containers.

Take apart the Bic Pen; you want the white barrel part, and you can discard the rest. Straighten your pre-tabbed wicks to the best of your ability, taking in mind they do not have to be perfectly vertical. Insert the wick through the barrel of the pen– six-inch wicks are best. The barrel makes it easier to handle the wick.

While keeping the wick in the barrel, apply hot glue to the base of the wick tab. Using the barrel to guide the wick, press the tab into the center of your container. Remove the barrel from the wick. There are several videos on this if you have further questions or need a visual aid.

Step 3: Secure the wick top.

Using a clothespin, secure the wick top. Clothespins work best for containers with an open diameter of up to three inches. For a larger container, you may have to improvise something else.

The main objective is to support the wick– to keep it centered and as straight as possible while the wax cools. You can also wait to do this step after pouring the wax.

Step 4: Preheat your desired container.

Once the wax reaches the proper temperature and you have mixed all your additives, you'll want to preheat your desired containers to about 150 degrees Fahrenheit. You can use a heat gun, or you can do it in the oven at the lowest heat setting. If you are using a heat gun be careful since they can sometimes get hotter than 150 degrees Fahrenheit.

This step isn't exactly needed, but it can help improve the finished product since it will basically allow you to pour your wax without trapping bubbles and improving the wax's ability to adhere to the glass.

Step 5: Pouring the wax.

Once you wax reaches the proper temperature of 160 degrees Fahrenheit, you can proceed with your initial pouring. Carefully fill your heat-proof container to the desired level. If you plan to have a lid on your container remember to fill it to a level that allows enough room for the lid to properly fit on the candle once finished without crushing or bending the wick.

Save about 20 percent of the wax in your pouring pitcher for the next step. DO NOT return your wax to the heat source. Allow the wax to completely cool before you move on to the next step.

This will sometimes be six or more hours, so find yourself a movie you are yet to watch or a great book you have not had the time to read. Slow cooling is going to give you the best results for container candles so you shouldn't try to speed up the cooling process.

Step 6: Repour wax.

After the candle has cooled completely, you'll notice the wax has sunk a bit in the middle. With the wax set aside from the previous step, you should melt it back down to a temperature of 185 degrees Fahrenheit using the bain-marie.

This higher temperature will increase the adhesion between wax layers. Repour the liquid wax to a level that just barely covers the solid wax from the previous step. This will help hide seam lines. Allow the candle to cool completely.

Step 7: Trim the wick appropriately.

Once the candle is cooled completely and has solidified, remove the clothespin or other item supporting the wick and trim the wick to within ¼ inch of the candle.

You are now ready to use, gift, or sell your candle, but make sure you follow the following guidelines:

- ☐ Burn on a heat-resistant surface only since containers can break.
- ☐ Burn candles for no more than four hours at a time.
- ☐ Protect the candle from drafts.
- ☐ Keep the wick trimmed to ¼ inch from the candle at all times.
- ☐ Keep the candle out of reach of children and pets.
- ☐ Never move a candle while it is burning or while there is melted wax in it.
- ☐ Keep the candle away from any flammable objects.
- ☐ Never allow a burning candle to be unattended.

MAKING VOTIVE CANDLES

Votive candles are probably one of the easiest you can choose to make. They can be used in a variety of settings and burn for about 15 hours while using up nearly all of the wax you used to create it.

This is helpful when it comes to throwing the scent. Since they aren't meant to be free-standing candles, they should only be burned in a holder designed for burning votive candles.

For this basic recipe you'll need the following:

☐ Wax suitable for votive candles.

☐ Wax additives if needed for wax formulation.

☐ Desired fragrance oil.

☐ Desired colored dye.

☐ Pre-tabbed wicks are suitable for votive candles.

☐ Metal votive molds.

☐ Mold release spray.

☐ Pouring pot.

☐ Thermometer.

The following is the process to make a basic votive candle.

Step 1: Prepare the wax mixture.

Set up your bain-marie to melt the wax. An ideal temperature for votive candles is 175 degrees Fahrenheit. Once your wax is completely melted, you can mix any additives you need in the following order while trying to avoid introducing too much air to the mixture:

1. Any needed additives such as stearic acid.
2. Any desired fragrance oil.
3. Any desired colored dye.

Before pouring your wax, you may choose to lightly coat the molds with a thin film of mold release agents like a silicone spray or a Pam style cooking spray. This helps to easily release the finished candle, although it is often only needed with new molds.

Step 2: The first wax pouring.

Set up a newspaper-lined surface under your votive molds to catch any spills. Once your wax is at the proper pouring temperature of 175 degrees Fahrenheit, fill your mold to the lip. The goal is to fill the entire mold without overflowing. Filling too low can result in a seam line on your finished candle. Be careful to avoid as many bubbles as possible when pouring your wax. Save about 20 percent of your wax for the next step and don't return it to the heat source just yet.

Step 3: Add your wicks.

Allow the wax to cool for a short time. While cooling, straighten your wicks a bit once the wax is starting to congeal, then you can insert your wicks. The tab will stick to the bottom when it touches. Try to position them in the center part of the mold.

It is important that you wait for the congealing phase. At this point, the wax is cool enough that it won't affect the firmness of the wick while still allowing the metal tab to stick to the mold base. At higher temperatures, it is harder to manage the wick.

Once the tab is stuck to the mold base, you can manipulate the wick to straighten it more if it needs the adjustment. While the candle cools, the wax may shrink and pull the wick off center. If this happens, simply tug the wick occasionally. Be careful not to use too much force, so the metal tab doesn't come free of the base. Allow the wax to cool completely before proceeding to the next step– this can take between three to four hours.

Step 4: Second wax pouring.

Once your wax is completely cool it will have shrunk slightly, leaving a slight hole that needs to be filled. Meltdown the wax saved from the previous step. The temperature this time should be 10 to 15 degrees hotter than the first pouring or about 190 degrees Fahrenheit. This will help adhere the two layers. Once the wax is at the appropriate temperature, you can pour and fill the mold to just above the lip. Try to avoid any spills, and allow the candles to cool completely.

Step 5: Remove the candle from the mold.

After the wax is completely cooled, you can remove the candles from their molds. Typically they will slide out without difficulty if they are completely cool and fully solidified. Otherwise, they may be more difficult to remove.

You can place them in the freezer for five minutes if they decide not to cooperate. You are now ready to enjoy your votive candles, and make sure you burn them in a votive holder when the time comes along.

MAKING PILLAR CANDLES

Next up is the molded pillar candle. The fun part of making pillar candles is that there are several different sizes and shapes to choose from. The molds here are made out of sheet metal, aluminum, and occasionally plastic, latex or silicone.

The most common types of molds are made out of sheet metal since they are durable and will often last for years without a lot of maintenance. The following instructions are focused on using sheet metal molds.

For this basic recipe you'll need the following:

- ☐ Wax.
- ☐ Desired fragrance oil.
- ☐ Desired colored dye.
- ☐ Metal pillar mold.
- ☐ Wick.
- ☐ Wick screw.
- ☐ Wick rod or a wooden skewer.
- ☐ Mold sealer putty.

The following is the process for making a basic pillar candle.

Step 1: Prepare the wax mixture.

Set up a bain-marie to start melting your wax. While the wax is melting, move on to the next steps; but keep a close eye on your wax.

Step 2: Thread the wick through the wick hole.

Choose a wick that is of the proper size for the chosen diameter intended for the mold that you will be making. Pass the wick through the wick hole at the base of the mold. Try dipping the end of the wick in some molten wax and carefully rolling it through your fingers if the end is frayed so it will form a nice pointed tip.

Step 3: Secure the wick to the wick rod.

While keeping the wick within the wick hole, tie one end to the wick rod. You can use a special wick rod or a simple wooden skewer. The function of any tool is the same, so it does not matter what you use as long as it gets the job done without much of a struggle.

Step 4: Secure the wick to the wick hole.

Use a wick screw to secure the wick– for this you will need a Phillips screwdriver. Make sure you leave the screw a little bit on the loose end, so it doesn't cut the wick or damage the mold by being too tight. The main purpose of this screw is to keep the wick from sliding back through the hole; it isn't meant to seal the hole.

The wick needs to be taut, but not to the point that it causes the mold to warp. Trim the wick to the point so that you leave about half to one inch of wick.

Step 5: Seal the wick hole.

Using your mold sealer, seal the wick hole along with the screw and wick. This will prevent the molten wax from leaking. Press the sealer in place firmly to make sure you have a tight seal. You might want to lightly wind the wick around the screw before you apply the sealer. In the end, you shouldn't be able to see any parts of the wick.

Step 6: First wax pouring.

Once the wax has reached the appropriate temperature of 175 to 185 degrees Fahrenheit you can add your fragrances and dyes in the following order:

1. Any needed additives to maintain a solid structure.
2. Desired fragrance oil.
3. Desired colored dyes.

Mix all your additives well with a wooden spoon. Once everything is completely mixed, and at the right temperature, you can pour the wax into your prepared candle mold. Be sure to have an old towel or some paper towels on hand for any spills.

Fill the mold to about half an inch from the top. Leave some wax in the pouring pot for a later step, but don't place it back on the heat source yet.

Step 7: Place relief holes.

Allow the candle to cool a bit until a film forms on the surface of the wax. Now you should poke some relief holes into the base of the candle to help with the natural shrinkage that happens as the wax solidifies. Ideally, the relief holes should be around the wick and need to be at a depth of about one inch less than the candle depth.

The exact number of relief holes doesn't matter, as the main purpose is to provide a vent. This vent allows the contracting volume of wax to suck air through in order to make up for the reduced volume. Without relief holes, several things can happen: air cavities may form within the candle, the wick may get off center, or the external walls of the candle can be deformed.

There may be a need to poke relief holes a few times during the cooling process in order to make sure the vent stays open and clear. Ensuring the vents are clear will also make it easier to fill in the voids later. Allow the candle to cool entirely before you move on to the next step.

This process can take several hours and sometimes even a full day for very large candles. Proceed to the next step when the candle is at room temperature.

Step 8: Second wax pouring.

Start by re-melting the wax you set aside. The temperature should be about five to ten degrees hotter than the original wax temperature. This will help the layers adhere to each other without much of a seam. Once the wax has reached the proper temperature, you can fill the sinkholes in your candle.

Fill it to a level just below that of the first filling. Filling higher than this will cause a horizontal seam line that will be visible from the exterior of the finished candle. Overfilling can also cause the wax to leak between the mold and the candle, resulting in an uneven finish.

Allow the candle to completely cool again before going to the next step.

Step 9: Remove the mold.

Start by removing the mold sealer and the wick screw. As long as the candle is completely cooled, the solid wax should slide out easily. If the candle doesn't slide out, place it in the refrigerator for about 15 minutes and try again. The cold will help the wax shrink more and help it separate from the mold.

The end of the candle attached to the wick rod is the bottom of the candle. Trim the wick on this end, so it is flush with the straight base of the candle. You can also level the base of the candle if you want by placing it on a previously heated cookie sheet. The heated cookie sheet will melt away some of the wax until you have a flat base. Trim the other side of the wick– the top wick– to about a quarter of an inch.

You are now ready to bask in the lovely scent and warm light of your candle. Remember to only burn them in designated candle holders and avoid drafts. Keep away from pets and children while burning and never leave a lit candle unattended.

MAKING SOY CONTAINER CANDLES

When you first get started making candles, it can be best to stick with regular wax before moving into making candles from other types of more temperamental wax. It can be easy to get confused by the numerous types of candle waxes available on the market.

So how can you choose the right one to use when you want to move out of standard wax candles and try you had at a more unique candle? There are typically two factors to consider when choosing a wax for your candle-making sprees.

1. The type of candle you are going to make– such as a pillar, votive or container.
2. Your own or your customers' personal preferences.

Paraffin is the most common type of candle wax and is often the traditional choice for making candles. This wax typically has a strong scent throw* and maintains color well. However, paraffin is made from petroleum oil, which is a non-renewable resource.

On the other hand, soy wax is made from soybean oil (a more environmentally-friendly option), and it is typically blended with natural botanical oils, so it is a great alternative to the traditional wax candle.

*Scent throw: the fragrance a candle has. It is split up into hot and cold, as each temperature will have a different scent.

Consider some of the following benefits available if you choose to make your candles from soy wax:

- It is both natural and renewable.
- Your candle will end up with a creamy pastel look.
- The fragrance oils bind easily into soy wax at a rate of two ounces of scents per pound of wax.
- Soy wax is often available in a convenient flake form that is faster to melt and easier to store.
- The selling market also expands, since soy oil also has moisturizing properties so that it can be used in massage candles or other bath and body recipes as well.

This isn't to say that this should be your go-to wax of choice. There are some disadvantages to soy wax that you want to consider carefully before making your candles with it.

- Soy wax often has a "frosting" appearance that may not be exactly what you or your sellers are looking for in the finished result.

- This kind of wax is more viscous so it will need a larger wick size in order to burn properly and cannot be shaped into many other forms.
- Even though it can hold more scented oils, that's because it naturally has a weaker scent throw than paraffin wax.
- Because it is so smooth, soy wax makes it difficult to get a deep and vibrant color without adding ridiculous amounts of colored dyes.

If you think you want to give soy wax a try, consider the following steps to help you make your candles.

Necessary Supplies:

☐ Soy Wax
☐ Containers for Soy Wax
☐ Wicks
☐ Bain-Marie System
☐ Thermometer
☐ Hot Glue or Wick Stickers
☐ Wick Holder Bars or any Wick Centering Tool
☐ Fragrance Oil of your choice
☐ Liquid Candle Dye of your choice
☐ Scale

Process:

Start by measuring the amount of wax you need for your containers in your pouring pitcher and melt the wax using your bain-marie system. The best way to measure your wax accurately is using a precision scale. Use an online calculator to help you determine how much wax you need for your containers. A thermometer comes in to monitor the temperature of the wax as it melts.

As the wax melts, you can prepare your wicks and containers. Determine the size of wick you need based on your containers and wax type. Soy waxes often need a wick about one to two sizes larger than those used for paraffin wax.

However, there are many variables that influence the way a candles burns, so you want to test your wicks. Secure the wick to the container bottoms with hot glue or wick stickers and use your choice of wick centering tools to keep the wick in place at the top.

Once your wax has reached a temperature of 170 to 175 degrees Fahrenheit, you can add your fragrance and dye, ensuring they are mixed in thoroughly. For a strong scent throw, you should use about 1.5 ounces of fragrance per pound of wax– or nine percent– and liquid dyes are best to use over dye chips since they provide greater concentration. Remove the wax from the heat and allow it to cool while stirring occasionally.

For soy wax, you should pour it into the containers once it reaches a temperature of between 100 and 150 degrees Fahrenheit, so 130 is often a good starting point.

The ideal pouring temperature depends on several factors including the type of soy wax you are using and the temperature of the environment around you. It is best to try out different pouring temperatures and find one that works for you.

Finally, allow the candles to cool entirely and trim the wicks to about a quarter of an inch. Your candles are now ready to be used. To get the best scent throw, you should allow the candles to sit for several days before using, so the oils bind with the wax.

Soy candles can experience a unique thing known as frosting, which doesn't occur with other types of wax. Frosting happens when your soy candle develops white spots on its surface either right away or over time. This is a normal condition of soy candles. Here are a few things you can do to control frosting:

- Leaving the candle uncolored or dyeing it very light cream-hued shades in order to camouflage the white spots.
- Purchase soy wax that contains specific natural botanical oils that assist in reducing frosting. The downside is that those same oils also diminish the scent throw, so the candle would require a lot more fragrance oils to make up for it.
- Mixing paraffin wax with soy wax.
- Determining the right pouring temperature and/or preheating your containers. However, the frosting will still appear over time.

Now, most people who regularly purchase soy candles are already used to the frost spots, so they will most likely not mind as long as the quality of your product is great. However, it is up to you to use whichever wax you prefer.

MAKING BEESWAX CANDLES

Another great natural option for making candles is beeswax. Typically, these candles don't have an added scent or dye, but they can help provide variety and uniqueness to your candle line.

Supplies:

- ☐ Filtered Beeswax
- ☐ Coconut Oil
- ☐ Canning Jars

☐ Cotton Braided Wicks

☐ A Bain-Marie System

☐ Skewers

Process:

Before starting, it is important to note that beeswax can be very difficult to remove from surfaces. So make sure you have a specific set of tools for working with it and prepare your surface to protect it. In addition, you can also use these tools for other beeswax products such as lotions, face masks, soaps, and so on

Start by setting your beeswax in a pitcher or other container for your bain-marie setup. Place the pitcher in your bigger pot with enough water to come up the outside of the pitcher without spilling into it. Remember that the water will eventually boil, so you should not fill it so high that the water will bubble over into the pitcher.

Bring the water to a boil, lower the heat, then maintain a gentle boil until all of the beeswax melts.

While the beeswax is melting, you can prepare your wicks. Cut three or four wicks up to six inches long.

Once the beeswax is completely melted, remove it from the heat and add in the coconut oil. Stir gently with the skewer until the oil is melted and well mixed with the beeswax.

Pour a small amount of wax into each jar or container that you are using so you have about a half inch covering the bottom of the jar/container. Return the pitcher to the hot water to make sure the wax stays melted.

Place a wick down into the wax at the center of each container. You can use a skewer to push down the wick and hold it there for a few minutes to make sure it is correctly placed. Allow the wax to cool until it is solid enough to keep the wick in place, or about five to ten minutes.

Wrap the top end of the wick around a skewer until taut, then leave the skewer resting across the top of the jar, so the wick remains centered and straight.

You may need to use a small piece of tape to keep the wick from sliding off the skewer.

Hold the skewer while pouring the remaining melted wax into each container. Leave about an inch of space at the top of each container. Reposition the wick as needed so that it stays within the center of the container.

Allow the wax to cool entirely. This can sometimes take up to several hours, but ideally, you should let the candles sit overnight. Trim the wick to about a half inch; don't trim the wick any shorter than this because anything shorter will make a smaller frame that will likely tunnel the candle.

If the candle flickers a lot or smoke, you should blow it out, trim the wick some more, and try relighting. During your first burn, you should ideally keep it lit for two and a half hours or until the entire surface is melted.

When working with beeswax, use caution as it is highly flammable. Don't allow the beeswax to get too hot or to spill on a hot stove. Otherwise this could become a fire hazard, and that is where the fire extinguisher would come in.

MAKING WAX MELTS

Wax melts are essentially a cube of scented wax that is placed into a tart warmer or tart burner which gently melts the wax and releases the fragrance. These resulting scents can last hours to days. Once the wax melt is finished, the remaining wax is discarded, and new cubes can be added as desired.

Nearly any kind of paraffin or soy wax can be used to make wax melts. The main thing is to avoid waxes that are soft or sticky since they can be both messy and difficult to remove from the mold packaging; harder waxes are often easier to remove. It is best to choose a wax that has a melting point of 145 degrees Fahrenheit or less so that the wax melts smoothly and evenly in a tart warmer.

You can calculate how much wax you need by using the general rule of thumb: one pound of wax will fill a six-cavity tart mold. You should add your fragrance at a rate of three to nine percent by weight. Your objective is to get about six percent fragrance load since this comes out to about one ounce of fragrance oil per pound of wax.

To make fragrance melts you'll need the following supplies:

- ☐ Wax
- ☐ Desired fragrance oil
- ☐ Desired colored dye
- ☐ Six-cavity tart molds
- ☐ Pouring Pitcher
- ☐ Bain-Marie
- ☐ Heat source
- ☐ Thermometer

☐ Wooden spoon

☐ Scale

The following is the process for making basic wax melts:

Step 1: Measure your wax.

Start by measuring one pound of wax on a digital scale.

Step 2: Melt your wax.

Using a bain-marie or other wax melting setup, melt your wax to a temperature of 175 degrees Fahrenheit. The bain-marie is best since indirect heat will be the safest way to melt wax evenly. Either way, always monitor the temperature of your wax and never leave it unattended.

Step 3: Add the desired coloring.

Once at your appropriate temperature, remove the wax from the heat source. Add any desired colored dye and mix thoroughly.

Step 4: Add the desired fragrance oil.

Add any fragrance oil you want. It is best to add about an ounce of fragrance oil to a pound of wax in order to get a six percent fragrance load. Mix the oil in thoroughly by stirring well with the wooden spoon.

Step 5: Pour the wax.

Once you have added your dyes and fragrances, allow your wax to cool until it reaches a pouring temperature of 150 to 160 degrees Fahrenheit. You should avoid pouring while the wax is too hot since it can melt the tart mold.

You should pour while the wax is as cool as possible, but should still be about 15 to 20 degrees Fahrenheit above the melting point. This can also help you avoid cosmetic blemishes in your wax melts.

Step 6: Cool and enjoy.

Allow the wax melts to cool for about an hour or two before you handle them. Then you are ready to enjoy them in a designed tart warmer or tart burner.

Now that we know the basics of making various types of candles let's look at how you can develop scents for them. Scents are important since they can set a mood, influence an occasion, and even serve some medicinal purposes.

There is a specific way to mix fragrances to get exactly the blend you are looking for.

CHOOSING CANDLE FRAGRANCES

A beautifully-crafted candle with an elegant fragrance can do wonders for the ambiance of a room. Certain smells can take us to another place– they can inspire and relax us in a single whiff. The scent is a powerful sense and serves to trigger our memories.

No matter what goal you want to achieve, scent can help you. So how do the professionals come up with the right blends for candles? Let's start by looking at what you should consider when deciding what fragrance to use for your candles.

FACTORS THAT HELP DECIDE SCENT

ROOM SPACE

The first thing you want to consider is how you want the scent to affect your space. While candles may work in most rooms, they can also present a safety hazard in other rooms. Candles provide extra warmth to their surroundings and make for a comforting atmosphere in a living room or dining room, but they can be a hazard in a bathroom if they are placed next to flammable items, or a front hallway.

Before you choose a scent that works, you need to think about the space where it is most likely going to be used.

KNOW WHAT SCENTS PEOPLE LIKE

The scent is also something that can be very personal. What you may think is a great scent, most people may not want in a candle that burns in their home. Therefore, you need to base your fragrance choice on the preferences of those who are going to be purchasing and using your candles.

Chose a scent that is known to affect a mood or invoke a specific memory so you can offer a widely-accepted good scent for people. Consider the following types that people tend to prefer when choosing scents for your candles:

Floral - Whether light or heavy, popular floral fragrances typically include rose, lavender, lilac, freesia, and jasmine.

Woody - Typically a rich and natural option popularly made from sandalwood, cedar, moss, and patchouli.

Citrus - A bright and fresh scent typically made from orange, grapefruit, and lemon.

Fruity - A sweet one made from scents like peach and blackberry.

Fresh - Often light with aquatic hints. It often brings out the aroma of fresh and clean linens.

Green - Natural and herby. Typically made from grass type scents.

Spicy - A warm and rich scent that is typically made from cinnamon, pepper, ginger, clove, and nutmeg.

Sweet - Often like baking goods fresh out of the oven. Typical scents used in this category are vanilla and almond.

MOOD AND TIME OF YEAR

The scent is a wonderful way to change the atmosphere of a room to match the season. In the spring and summer, your house can benefit from light and fresh scent while a winter or fall scent is typically heavy and spicy. Many fragrances are labeled by what they desire to achieve more than their actual scent, so keep this in mind when designing the scents for your candles.

Now that we know what goes into choosing your candle scents, it is important also to understand what fragrance is and how various aromas blend together. To do this, we need to consider and understand the fragrance wheel. Let's look at this next.

THE FRAGRANCE WHEEL

When it comes to combining fragrances for your candles, it can be a little daunting. You're not alone; it is also overwhelming for even the most experienced candle makers. There are many options when it comes to choosing a fragrance, even in the fact that you can use essential oils, fragrance oils and/or raw ingredients for natural scents.

There are always staple scents that everyone puts together, and these are the ones people easily identify, but it can also be a good idea to experiment and try to come up with something different that people haven't experienced before to give you an edge over the competition.

The scent is much like the color in that it has categories to help you determine what blends will work well together. The fragrance wheel is similar to the color wheel in the fact that is displays the four main categories of scents and their subcategories.

https://www.bulkapothecary.com/blog/wp-content/uploads/2014/04/Screen-Shot-2014-04-01-at-10.41.33-AM.png

There are three basic rules to follow when blending scents:

1. Side by side fragrances on the chart blend well together.
2. Selecting opposites on the wheel can complement each other.
3. Selecting three fragrances that form a triangle when looking at the wheel will often complement each other as well.

Once you choose a few fragrances from the wheel, you can test your blending scent. To do this, you need the following supplies:

- ☐ Your desired essential or fragrance oils.
- ☐ A small jar with an airtight lid.
- ☐ Clean cotton swabs for each scent oil you want to blend.
- ☐ A notebook for keeping track of results.

Next, you need to have a basic understanding of fragrance notes and how to build a scent.

THREE FRAGRANCE NOTES

All fragrance oils have a top, middle, and bottom or base notes. Perfumers used these terms when they describe fragrances. The notes are based on the evaporation rate of the scent of the oil itself.

Top Notes

A thin fragrance oil with a large, sharp, and fresh scent that you will smell first before it evaporates. It is recommended that this scent takes up five to 20 percent of the blend.

Middle Notes

The main body of the scent that helps to balance the top and bottom notes. It is recommended this be 50 to 80 percent of the blend.

Bottom Notes

A deep, warm, and heavy scent. This smell lingers the longest in the fragrance. It should typically make up 5 to 20 percent of the blend.

Blends that often include a top, middle, and bottom note are going to be more complex to make, but this also makes them more inspiring and appealing to people. There are some scents such as lavender that can be used as both a top and middle note and peppermint which can be a middle and bottom note.

So now that you know the basics, you can get started with blending scents. This can be the scary part since you'll end up wasting any fragrance oil that doesn't blend well, but remember it is all part of the learning curve.

We learn from our mistakes, particularly when dealing with the science of aromas. In order to save some money on more supplies, you should start by mixing only small amounts of fragrance oils and keeping track of the recipes and ratios in a notebook.

Once you find a blend you are satisfied with, work your way up to larger batches using the notes you took down while making it.

OIL RATIO TABLE

When creating larger formulas, you need to use drop ratios. For example, a one-ounce bottle of fragrance oil is 30 ml. Pipettes are easily used to measure up to 3 ml amounts, so you will need 10 whole pipettes to create a one-ounce bottle.

When testing ratios, it is best to use them in one-ounce formulas to ensure you are getting consistent results before doing a larger batch. This is a basic example of the math of moving from a drop ratio into a formula:

Drop Ratio	Ounce Ratio (10 Pipettes)
1 drop	1 pipette = 3 ml
9 drops	9 pipettes = 27 ml

Once all parts of the fragrance ratio are added to the bottle, swish them around to make sure they are fully blended. As you do this, make sure you take notes in your notebook so you can duplicate a scent that comes out well or improve one that did not work.

To create unique scents use the following steps:

Mix basic, foolproof components that always work well together as your base, and then use these to build into more complex blends. You can choose any combination of essential or fragrance oils you want. Go for components that have at least one top note, middle note, and bottom note, or just a few oils that you think will go well together.

The process of finding a fragrance is all about experimenting, as we have established. It is all about trial and error.

Start by opening the oils and the small glass jar. You may be able to get a good enough preview simply by having all the scents open at the same time.

One at a time, dip the tip of a clean cotton swab into the fragrance or essential oil. Use the lip of the bottle to squeeze any excess oil from the swab.

Place the swabs in the glass jar.

Repeat this process for each of the scents that you want to add into the fragrance blend.

Ensure you write down all oil scents you use and the amounts in your notebook.

Step away from the jar and take a few minutes to let the scent dissipate.

Return to the jar and gently sniff the area above it. This is the scent that you'll get at the early stages of the blend development. In the notebook write down your thoughts on the scent and answer two questions:

1. Is one scent overpowering the others?
2. Do two scents seem too similar to separate into distinct scents?

Place the lid on the jar and leave it in a cool, dark place. Let the jar sit for a few hours and then return to smell the blend again. This scent will have mixed more and had time to mature. Write down additional notes about the scent in your notebook. Repeat this process after sealing the jar and letting it rest in the same conditions as before for 48 hours. That period of time allows the aroma to be fully matured and completely mixed.

At this point, you can make any corrections to the blend. Perhaps add more of certain scents or try a different combination and repeat the above process.

Once you have a fragrance that you feel more than comfortable with you can consider trying it in a candle recipe. Take notes on this experiment as well to know whether you want to keep this recipe or try for a different scent next time.

When it comes to smelling fragrances there are a few things to keep in mind:

1. Try to get the same amount of essential or fragrance oil on each cotton swab and ensure the swabs are completely clean before dipping them. Otherwise, you can risk contaminating your oils and altering the scent.

2. Instead of cotton swabs, you can use an eye dropper or disposable pipette and a paper towel. Just remember to use a fresh dropper or pipette for each oil to avoid contamination.

3. Don't hold the jar up to your nose to smell the scent, rather let the scent rise up to you from the jar as it would with a candle.

4. Cleanse your scent receptors by sniffing coffee beans or ground coffee. Doing this between tests will help you get a more accurate reading of the scents you are testing.

5. Lastly, don't be afraid to experiment and try even some of the oddest combinations or those that don't exactly follow the strict top-middle-bottom note pattern. And no matter what, make sure you keep good notes.

Now that we know how we can make and blend essential or fragrance oils, let's consider some combination ideas to help you get started. Another thing that is important to understand is scent throw and how it can affect your candles.

CANDLE SCENT THROW

There are several factors to consider when it comes to trying to find that strong and lasting scent that is unique and makes your candle stand out from the others. You are faced with comparing scents from a variety of sources to see which is the strongest.

You'll also need to experiment with how the same aromas are impacted by different types of wax and additives. As you can tell, the list of variables for how a candle will smell is a long one. Perhaps the one constant is that you can use your nose to assess the good and bad smells. However, when it comes to scent intensity, you need to learn about scent throw. How you are able to compare intensity and scent throw, you may ask? It isn't that hard, but before we get started,

I want to take the time to help you realize you can trust your sense of smell and perhaps understand what exactly scent is telling you.

The sensory systems of your body all have common features including hearing, sight, smell, touch, and taste. All of these systems take a stimulus and turn it into an electrical signal that travels by nerves to eventually get to the brain where the information is then processed. After that point, the brain has a lot of work to do to process all of the signals from the various sensory inputs. Thankfully, there is a thing called sensory adaptation.

Sensory adaptation takes place when the sensory receptors reduce and eventually stop sending signals to the brain after the sensors are exposed to a constant stimulus for an extended period of time. This doesn't mean they stop functioning completely, but rather that they have achieved the threshold of activation.

If a more intense sensory stimulus occurs, the sensors will trigger and send a signal to the brain. Yet, if a low-intensity stimuli occurs, it won't trigger the sensor receptors to send a signal to the brain. In other words, the process of sensory adaptation can act as a filter for the sensory input system and helps to get rid of any constants in the environment around you.

Let's consider a quick example of sensory adaptation. At some point, you've likely had a bright light shined directly into your eyes. Once the light is removed, you'll notice that your eyes have difficulty picking up objects located in dim areas.

Basically, your threshold level for the photoreceptor cells is now raised, and they are less sensitive to light stimulation. You'll be able to spot items in the dim light as soon as your eyes adapt to the darkness again.

The same thing happens to your nose. Once you've been exposed to an odor for a long time, the scent receptors in your nose that have been associated with that odor will increase the activation threshold, and a signal will no longer be sent to the brain. Through this, your brain will no longer get a signal that tells it you are smelling frosted carrot cake, for instance, unless you expose those scent receptors to a stimulus that is more intense.

Now that you know more than you likely want to know about your sensory system let's discuss what this has to do with candle scent and scent throws.

Here's an example of two candles, A and B. Let's assume they are both scented for a Frosted Carrot Cake fragrance, and both are scented to the point that they smell like the real thing. They both probably seem to have a really good scent throw and can effectively cover an entire room in your home with their fragrance.

However, let's assume that these two candles are also different in some small way. Perhaps they were made with different additives, or the fragrance oils were made from different sources. What you are trying to determine is which one has the best scent throw; in other words, which scent is more intense. This part is now easier since we know about sensory adaptation.

The first thing you want to do is compare cold throw. To do this take large whiffs directly from the candle surface. Inhale Candle A deeply into your nose a few times. Then do the same with Candle B before returning to Candle A. Repeat this process a few times.

Eventually, sensory adaptation will occur, and you'll only be able to smell the more intense candle. The weaker candle will fall below the threshold that is needed to trigger the scent receptors in your nose.

Comparing the hot throw of candles is done in much a similar way, except you need to be careful to avoid burning the hairs in your nose or your head. Light both candles at the same time and allow them to burn for a few hours, so there is a decent melt pool in both. Extinguish the flame by dipping it into the melt pool– this will extinguish the flame without any smoke.

The hot throw is now emitted by the melt pool and not the flame. Plus, you'll have removed the extremely uncomfortable hazard of burning your nose hairs. From a distance above each candle, take a whiff of each and alternate between them.

The weaker candle will have a scent that falls below the threshold for your scent response, and you'll easily be able to identify the more intense candle.

As you can see, it is very easy to compare scent throw. Now you know how to compare candles, blend scents, choose the best wax for your and your client's personal needs, and every single other technicality for your candle-making experiences.

This is the best time for you to experiment with everything you have learned so far, along with variables such as additives, wax, curing time, and other things that can influence the scent throw of your finished candles.

It is also important to note that it can be difficult to smell your own candles for several days after you've made them. This is because sensory adaptation occurs when you are exposed to the scent while making the candles, so remember to keep your coffee beans near you.

FRAGRANCE OIL COMBINATIONS FOR CANDLES

AROMATHERAPY BLENDS

One of the more popular uses for candles or wax melts is that of aromatherapy. Burning a scented candle or wax melt is a great way to get some added medicinal perks. Consider trying some of the following aromatherapy fragrance blends for your next project if you want some specific health benefits.

6 Most Popular Healing Aromatherapy Blend Ideas

For calming scents to help with controlling anger or frustration consider some of the following blends:

- Patchouli and Orange
- Bergamot, Ylang Ylang, and Jasmine
- Chamomile, Bergamot, and Orange

For insomnia issues the following blend is excellent:

- Chamomile, Sage, and Bergamot

To help increase your energy consider any of the following blends:

- Frankincense, Lemon, and Peppermint
- Bergamot and Rosemary

- Basil, Cypress, and Grapefruit
- Ginger and Grapefruit

To help reduce the stress you can use one of the following blends:

- Grapefruit, Jasmine, and Ylang Ylang
- Lavender, Lemon, and Sage
- Bergamot, Frankincense, and Geranium

To help boost your confidence, you can consider any of the following blends:

- Orange and Rosemary
- Bergamot and Jasmine
- Cypress and Grapefruit

To help increase happiness consider the following blends:

- Grapefruit, Neroli, Rose, and Ylang Ylang
- Bergamot, Rose, and Sandalwood
- Frankincense, Geranium, and Orange

If you don't need an aromatherapy candle, but just want an enjoyable scent for any specific occasion, there are numerous options for you to choose from. Consider the following list of fragrance mixing ideas to help you come up with a good combination of your own:

- ☐ Summer Breeze: Lavender, Vanilla and Spring Rain

- ☐ Almond Joy: Chocolate, Coconut Cream, and Almond

- ☐ Angel Cake: Warm Sugar, Orange Blossom, Vanilla

- ☐ Anise and Cream: Anise and Vanilla

- ☐ Rosewood: Rose and Sandalwood

- ☐ Cinnamon Apples: Apple and Cinnamon

- ☐ Fruity Apple: Apple and Grapefruit

- ☐ Apple Jacks: Apple, Cinnamon, and Grapefruit

- ☐ Apple Rose: Apple and Rose

- ☐ Spiced Apple: Apple, Cinnamon, Bayberry and Hot Apple Pie
- ☐ Vanilla Apple: Apple and Vanilla
- ☐ Autumn Harvest: Pumpkin, Allspice, and Apple
- ☐ Autumn Spice: Orange and Cloves
- ☐ Baby Fresh: Baby Powder, Lavender, and Lilac
- ☐ Baby Powder: Rose and Vanilla
- ☐ Baby's Breath: Vanilla and Jasmine
- ☐ Banana Toffee: Toffee and Banana
- ☐ Bayberry Paradise: Tropical Mix and Bayberry
- ☐ Berries and Cream: Vanilla, Strawberry, and Raspberry
- ☐ Berry Patch: Patchouli, Strawberry, and Raspberry
- ☐ Birthday Cake: Vanilla and Buttercream
- ☐ Biscotti: Almond Pastry and Fudge Brownie
- ☐ Black Cherry Toffee: Black Cherry, Almond, Caramel, and Coconut

- ☐ Blackberry Crumble: Blackberry and Crème Brulee
- ☐ Blue Hawaiian: Blueberry and Pineapple
- ☐ Blueberry Cheesecake: Blueberry and Cheesecake
- ☐ Blueberry Cobbler: Blueberry Muffin and French Vanilla
- ☐ Boudoir: Rose, Musk, Vanilla, and Sandalwood
- ☐ Cajun Cream: French Vanilla and Butterscotch Brulee
- ☐ Candy Cane: Peppermint and Strawberry
- ☐ Cappuccino: Coffee and Irish Mocha
- ☐ Caramel Apple: Caramel and Apple
- ☐ Caribbean Vacation: Caribbean Breeze and Ocean Dream
- ☐ Lavender Chamomile: Lavender and Chamomile
- ☐ Charleston: Cinnamon and Sandalwood
- ☐ Cherry Cheesecake: Cherry and Cheesecake

- ☐ Cherry Colada: Cherry, Pineapple, and Coconut Cream
- ☐ Cherry Fairy: Cherry and Cotton Candy
- ☐ Cherry Lemonade: Cherry and Lemon
- ☐ Cherry Vanilla: Cherry and Vanilla
- ☐ Chocolate Covered Cherries: Chocolate, Cherries, and Buttercream
- ☐ Chocolate Chip Cookies: Pie Crust and Fudge Brownie
- ☐ Cinnamon Vanilla: Cinnamon and Vanilla
- ☐ Cinnamon Berry: Bayberry and Cinnamon
- ☐ Cinnamon Rose: Cinnamon and Rose
- ☐ Coconut Cream Pie: Vanilla, Coconut Cream, and Pie Crust
- ☐ Coconut Lime Verbena: Coconut and Key Lime
- ☐ Cosmopolitan: Cranberry, Pink Sugar, and Lime
- ☐ Berry Basket: Blueberry, Raspberry, and Strawberry

- [ ] Cranberry Apple Cider: Apple and Spiced Cranberry

- [ ] Cranberry Bread: Cranberry, Maple Sugar, and Fresh Baked Bread

- [ ] Creamsicle: Orange and Vanilla

- [ ] Strawberries and Cream: Strawberry and Crème Brulee

- [ ] Cantaloupe and Cucumber: Cantaloupe and Cucumber

- [ ] Cucumber Melon: Cucumber and Melon

- [ ] Dusty Rose: Rose and Baby Powder

- [ ] Daily Energizer: Lemongrass and Peppermint

- [ ] French Vanilla: Amaretto and Vanilla

- [ ] Vanilla Coffee: Coffee and Vanilla

- [ ] Fresh Baked Pie: Buttercream and Pumpkin Spice

- [ ] Fuzzy Navel: Peach and Orange

- [ ] German Chocolate Cake: Fudge Brownie and Coconut Cream

☐ Ginger Pumpkin: Ginger, Nutmeg, Cinnamon, Amber, and Pumpkin

☐ Lemon Meringue Pie: Sweet Lemon Zest and Pie Crust

☐ Cucumber Green Tea: Cucumber and Green Tea

☐ Fruit Harvest: Apple, Orange Blossom, and Strawberry

☐ Hawaiian Paradise: Pineapple, Coconut, Mango, and Papaya

☐ Herbal Fusion: Patchouli and Gardenia

☐ Honeysuckle Peach: Peach and Honeysuckle

☐ Honeysuckle Rose: Rose and Honeysuckle

☐ Jazzy: Basil and Jasmine

☐ Key Lime Pie: Key Lime, Sweet Cream, and Pie Crust

☐ Lavender Lemon: Lavender and Lemongrass

☐ Lemon Pound Cake: Lemon, Freshly Baked Bread, Sweet Lemon Zest, and Vanilla

☐ Lemon Sage: Lemon and Sage

- Malibu: Blueberry, Strawberry and Cherry

- Mango Punch: Mango, Orange, and Lime

- Melon Punch: Cantaloupe, Watermelon, and Honeydew

- Mint Chocolate: Chocolate and Candy Cane or Peppermint Cream

- Mother Earth: Clove, Sandalwood, Oak, and Cedar

- New Car: Leather and Vanilla

- Ocean Breeze: Tropicana and Spring Rain

- Orange Spice: Orange, Clove, and Harvest Spice

- Passion Flower Chamomile: Passion Flower and Chamomile

- Peach Cobbler: Peach, Pie Crust, Vanilla, Maple Sugar, and Cinnamon

- Peach Pie: Peach, Vanilla, Warm Sugar, and Pie Crust

- Peaches and Cream: Vanilla, Sweet Cream, and Peach

- [ ] PB&J: Peanut Butter and Jelly, or Peanuts, Strawberry, and Freshly Baked Bread

- [ ] Peppermint Tea: Peppermint and Green Tea

- [ ] Peppermint Patty: Chocolate and Peppermint

- [ ] Piña Colada: Coconut Cream and Pineapple

- [ ] Pine Forest: Pine, Cedar, and Bayberry

- [ ] Pink Lemonade: Strawberry, Sugar, and Lemon

- [ ] Polynesian Paradise: Lavender and Ylang Ylang

- [ ] Floral Bouquet: Lilac, Lavender, and Gardenia

- [ ] Relaxation: Chamomile and Spearmint

- [ ] Peace: Lavender, Peppermint, and Green Tea

- [ ] Quiet: Patchouli, Rose, and Sandalwood

- [ ] Sea Breeze: Peppermint and Rain

- [ ] Gentle Rose: Rose and Vanilla

- [ ] Vanilla Spice: Vanilla and Allspice

- [ ] Strawberries and Cream: Strawberries and Vanilla

- [ ] Strawberry Cheesecake: Strawberry and Cheesecake

- ☐ Strawberry Daiquiri: Strawberry, Vanilla, and Piña Colada
- ☐ Strawberry Kiwi: Strawberry and Kiwi
- ☐ Strawberry Lemonade: Strawberry and Lemon
- ☐ Strawberry Shortcake: Strawberry and Angel Food Cake
- ☐ Strawberry Banana: Strawberry, Warm Sugar, and Banana
- ☐ Sugar Cookie: Butter Pecan and Crème Brulee
- ☐ Summer Rain: Spring Rain and Sunflower
- ☐ Peaceful Dreams: Lavender and Sweet Pea
- ☐ Tutti Frutti: Pear, Raspberry, Kiwi, Apple and Watermelon
- ☐ Vanilla Garden: Rose, Lavender, and Vanilla
- ☐ Vanilla Mocha: Vanilla, Coffee, Chocolate
- ☐ Wild Berries: Blueberry, Cherry, Raspberry, and Strawberries and Cream

SUMMER SEASON BLENDS

If you need to find specific scents for certain occasions then consider the following scents for a summer fragrance:

- ☐ Mint Mojito: Lime, Rum, and Peppermint Sugar

- ☐ Lemon Pound Cake: Lemon, French Vanilla, Warm Brown Sugar, Birthday Cake

- ☐ Cranberry Punch: Watermelon, Lemon, Hibiscus, and Cranberry

- ☐ Amaretto Sour: Amaretto, Lemon, Almond, and Cherry

- ☐ Tropical Oasis: Pineapple, Coconut Cream, and Hibiscus

- ☐ Peach Iced Tea: Lemon, Sweet Lemon Zest, and Peach

- ☐ Summer Delight: Peach, Citrus, and Hydrangea

- ☐ Sangria: Merlot, Orange Blossom, Sweet Lemon Zest, Cinnamon

- ☐ Root Beer Float: Vanilla, Cream, and Root Beer

- ☐ Strawberry Lemonade: Strawberry, Lemon, Sugar

- ☐ Pineapple Upside Down Cake: Pound Cake, Pineapple, and Maple Sugar

FALL SEASON BLENDS

For fall scents consider the following scent blend ideas:

- ☐ Peach Cobbler: Snickerdoodle and Peach

- ☐ Muscadine Wine: Merlot, Strawberries, and Muscadine

- ☐ Pumpkin Marshmallow: Marshmallow, Pumpkin, and Nutmeg.

- ☐ Chocolate Pie: Sugar Cookie, Sweet Cream, and Fudge Brownie

- ☐ Cranberry Apple Crumble: Cranberry, Cinnamon, and Baked Apple Pie

☐ Campfire Smores: Marshmallow, Chocolate, Warm Brown Sugar, Allspice, and Firewood

☐ Pumpkin Latte: Vanilla, Pumpkin, Cinnamon, Nutmeg, Allspice, and Coffee

☐ Hazelnut Latte: Vanilla and Hazelnut Coffee

WINTER SEASON BLENDS

For winter scents consider the following scent blend ideas:

☐ Peppermint Hot Chocolate: Hot Chocolate, Cinnamon, and Peppermint

☐ Christmas Pastry: Apple, Cinnamon Bread, Sweet Cream.

☐ Snow Blossom: Gardenia and Peppermint

SPRING SEASON BLENDS

For spring scents consider the following scent blend ideas:

- ☐ Pink Champagne: Chardonnay and Sugar Plum

- ☐ Spring Blossom: Cherry Blossom and Pink Chiffon

- ☐ Spring Flowers: Patchouli, Cardamom, and Vanilla

- ☐ Clothesline: Lavender, Cotton, and Linen

MASCULINE SCENT BLENDS (FOR HIM)

For masculine scents consider the following scent blend ideas

- ☐ Cowboy: Sandalwood and Leather

- ☐ Fresh: Eucalyptus and Citronella

- ☐ Gentleman: Smoked Cognac, Balsam

- ☐ Lumberjack: Cedarwood Spice and Coffee

- ☐ Adventurous Pirate: Driftwood, Sea Salt, and Rum

FEMININE SCENT BLENDS (FOR HER)

For feminine scents consider the following scent blend ideas:

- ☐ Aphrodite: Olive and Lemon Verbena
- ☐ Leather and Lace: Chamomile and Leather
- ☐ Southern Spark: Vanilla and Leather
- ☐ Beauty: Strawberries and Cream, Gardenia, and Rainforest
- ☐ Lace Beauty: Cashmere and Amber

SOME UNIQUE BLEND IDEAS

For some unique scents that can be used in a variety of settings consider the following scent blend ideas:

- ☐ Forest: Autumn Pear, Balsam, and Cedar
- ☐ Prairie: Fresh Cut Grass and Honeysuckle
- ☐ Winter Days: Cinnamon and Firewood
- ☐ Rice Krispies: Sugar Cookie and Marshmallow
- ☐ Lucky Charms: Marshmallow and Buttercream
- ☐ Irish Cream: Crème Brulee and Coffee

- [ ] Banana Pudding: Banana, Sweet Cream, and Sugar Cookie
- [ ] Tranquility: Iced Tea, Everglades, and Spearmint
- [ ] Calming: Mint and Lavender
- [ ] Peeps: Marshmallow, Cotton Candy, Vanilla
- [ ] Jelly Beans: Candy Apple, Raspberry, and Cherry Vanilla

LAST WORD

These scent blends are just some ideas to get you started. You'll want to experiment with the individual quantities of each scent depending on their strength and the combinations you intend to use. You can even add extra scents or remove scents as needed until you get a scent that appeals to you or your client.

You can also brainstorm and come up with your own scent blend ideas that provide a sense of individuality to your business or hobby. Perhaps you want to make a product line of candles inspired by a book, show, movie, biomes, food, or even country.

Just imagine: a golden candle scented like caramel to represent the golden Snitch in Harry Potter, or perhaps a creamy yellow candle scented like butterbeer. There also could be relaxation candles with more subtle scents intended to alleviate a specific ailment or to relieve stress.

If you want a more personal line, the candles could represent your loved ones, favorite things, or pets.

The possibilities are truly endless. So, get out there and start experimenting with making excellent scented candles!

Made in the USA
Middletown, DE
05 August 2020